First World War
and Army of Occupation
War Diary
France, Belgium and Germany

59 DIVISION
Divisional Troops
469 Field Company Royal Engineers
1 January 1916 - 29 February 1916

WO95/3017/3

The Naval & Military Press Ltd
www.nmarchive.com
Published in association with The National Archives

Published by

The Naval & Military Press Ltd

Unit 10 Ridgewood Industrial Park,

Uckfield, East Sussex,

TN22 5QE England

Tel: +44 (0) 1825 749494

www.naval-military-press.com

www.nmarchive.com

This diary has been reprinted in facsimile from the original. Any imperfections are inevitably reproduced and the quality may fall short of modern type and cartographic standards.

© **Crown Copyright**
Images reproduced by permission of The National Archives, London, England, 2015.

Contents

Document type	Place/Title	Date From	Date To
Heading	WO95/3017/3		
Heading	59 Div 469 Coy Re formerly 2/2 N Mid Fld Coy Re 1916 Jan-1916 Feb		
Heading	War Diary Of 2/2nd North Midland Field Company Royal Engineers From 1st January 1916 To 31st January 1916 Volume 1)		
War Diary	Radlett Hants:	01/01/1916	30/01/1916
Heading	War Diary Of 2/2nd N.M Field Coy RE 59th N.M Division From February 1st 1916 To February 29th 1916 (Volume 1)		
War Diary	Radlett	02/02/1916	29/02/1916

WO95
3017/3

59 DIV

469 COY RE

formerly

2/2 N MID FLD COY RE

1916 JAN — 1916 FEB

Confidential

War Diary

of

2/2nd North Midland Field Company Royal Engineers

From 1st January 1916 to 31st January 1916

(Volume 1)

WAR DIARY
or
INTELLIGENCE SUMMARY

Army Form C. 2118

Place	Date	Hour	Summary of Events and Information	Remarks and references to Appendices
Radlett Herts.	1916 Jan 1st		Strength of Company, 224 all ranks, 7 officers and 217 N.C.O.s and men, which includes 33 recruits of 1 month service.	A03
"	" 9th	2 PM.	1 Officer, 5 N.C.O.s and 18 men detailed to instruct infantry in field works:- 1 Officer 3 N.C.O.s and 12 men sent to 178th Infantry Brigade at WATFORD. 1 N.C.O. and 3 men " " 176th " " , ST ALBANS. 1 N.C.O and 3 men " " 177th " " , HARPENDEN.	A03
"	" 19th	5.30 AM	1 Officer 7 N.C.O.s & 14 men detailed for special duty in connection with WAR OFFICE	A03
"	" 30	4.30 PM	Infantry instruction party from WATFORD returned (1 officer 3 N.C.O.s & 12 men	A03

M.D.Bonwell Capt.
for O/C. 2/2nd North Midland Field Coy. R.E.

Confidential

War Diary

of

2/2nd N.M. Field Coy RE   59th N.M. Division

From February 1st 1916   to   February 29th 1916

(Volume 1.)

WAR DIARY 2/2nd N.M. Field Coy RE

Army Form C. 2118.

Instructions regarding War Diaries and Intelligence Summaries are contained in F. S. Regs., Part II. and the Staff Manual respectively. Title pages will be prepared in manuscript.

INTELLIGENCE SUMMARY.

(Erase heading not required.)

Hour, Date, Place	Summary of Events and Information	Remarks and references to Appendices
Radlett 2nd Feb 1916	1 Officer, 7 N.C.O.s & 14 men return from special duty in connection with WAR OFFICE	6/7/13
" 7th " "	1 Officer, 2 N.C.O.s & 14 men detailed to instruct 178th Infantry Brigade WATFORD in field works.	6/7/13
" 13th " "	Sec. Lieut: Harries & 1 man return from ALDERSHOT	6/7/13
" 14th " "	Lieut: Chinnery & 1 man proceed to ALDERSHOT for instruction in	6/7/13
" 19th " "	Infantry Instruction party from ST. ALBANS return. Received 50 rifles on loan from 177th Inf. Brigade HARPENDEN	6/7/13
" 20th " "	Infantry Instruction party from HARPENDEN return 1 N.C.O. & 3 men detailed to instruct 176th Inf Brigade ST. ALBANS in field works	6/7/13
	3 men detailed to instruct 177th Inf. Brigade HARPENDEN in field works	6/7/13
" 22nd " "	Sec. Lieut: J.G. Harries & 1 man proceed to S.W.E. Class DEGANWY	6/7/13
" 26th " "	Sec. Lieut: A.G. Clutterbuck & 1 man return from S.W.E. Class BRIGHTLINGSEA	6/7/13
	1 N.C.O. & 2 men detailed for instructional course in signalling at HEMEL HAMPSTEAD	
" 27th " "	Sec. Lieut: I.V. Wilcox 1 N.C.O. & 1 man proceed to S.W.E. Class BRIGHTLINGSEA	6/7/13
" 29th " "	Infantry instruction parties return from WATFORD, HARPENDEN & ST. ALBANS return	6/7/13
	Strength of Company 228 all ranks; 8 Officers & 220 N.C.O.s & men (3 men enlisted during the month)	

www.ingramcontent.com/pod-product-compliance
Lightning Source LLC
Chambersburg PA
CBHW081516160426
43193CB00014B/2709